JUNGLE BIRDS

Written by Anita Ganeri
Illustrated by Steve Lings
and Steve Weston

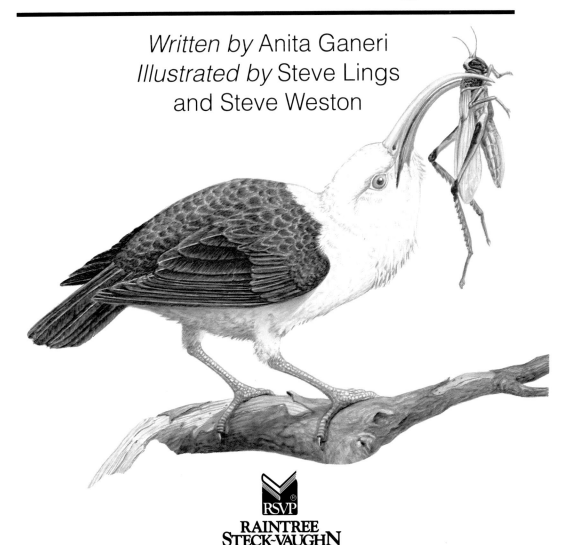

RSVP

**RAINTREE
STECK-VAUGHN**
P U B L I S H E R S
The Steck-Vaughn Company

Austin, Texas

Editor: Kim Merlino
Project Manager: Julie Klaus

Library of Congress Cataloging-in-Publication Data
Ganeri, Anita, 1961-
      Jungle birds / written by Anita Ganeri; illustrated by Steve Lings and
Steve Weston.
          p.   cm. — (Pointers)
      Includes index.
      Summary: Describes such jungle birds as the monkey-eating eagle,
toucan, and bird of paradise.
      ISBN 0-8114-6160-2
      1. Forest birds — Tropics — Juvenile literature. [1. Birds.   2. Jungle
animals.]   I. Lings, Steve, Ill.   II. Weston, Steve, Ill.   III. Title.
IV. Series.
QL695.5.G36   1994
598.29'152'0913—dc20   93-19869
                                                             CIP
                                                             AC

Printed and bound in the United States

1 2 3 4 5 6 7 8 9 0 VH 99 98 97 96 95 94 93

Foreword

This book is about the different types of birds which live in the jungle. "Jungle" is another word for the rain forests that grow along the equator in Central and South America, Africa, Asia, and parts of Australia and Papua New Guinea. These lush steamy forests are very hot. Because it rains frequently, they are also wet all year round. Jungles are rich in wildlife; more than half of all the world's species of plants and animals live in the rain forests. Among the animals are some of the most colorful and most unusual birds in the world.

Birds are warm-blooded, air-breathing animals. They all have beaks and lay eggs, usually in nests. Birds are the only animals whose bodies are covered with feathers. They all have wings, although not all birds can fly.

The trees in the rain forest form layers, according to their height above the ground. The tallest trees form what is called the emergent layer. These trees rise above the next highest layer of trees — the trees which make up the canopy. Below the canopy is the layer called the understory. Birds live in every layer and are also found foraging for food on the forest floor.

Contents

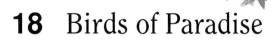

Monkey-eating Eagles

The huge monkey-eating eagle builds its nest among the crowns (tops) of the tallest rain forest trees, high up in the emergent layer. It is one of the fiercest and most powerful birds in the jungle. It flies through the canopy, searching for prey. When it spies a troop of monkeys, it pounces. It grasps a monkey in its vicelike claws and carries it back to its nest. One monkey is enough food for several days.

Each of the main areas of the world's rain forests has its own type of eagle. The monkey-eating eagle lives in Southeast Asia; the crowned eagle lives in Africa; and the harpy eagle lives in Central and South America.

3 Like all birds of prey, eagles have very good eyesight for spotting their prey among the leaves.

2 The eagle has a sharp, hooked beak which it uses for tearing meat apart. It also uses its beak to pull the fur from its prey before eating it.

1 The eagle feeds mainly on monkeys, flying lemurs, snakes, and large birds. It also steals poultry, pigs, and dogs from villages in the forest.

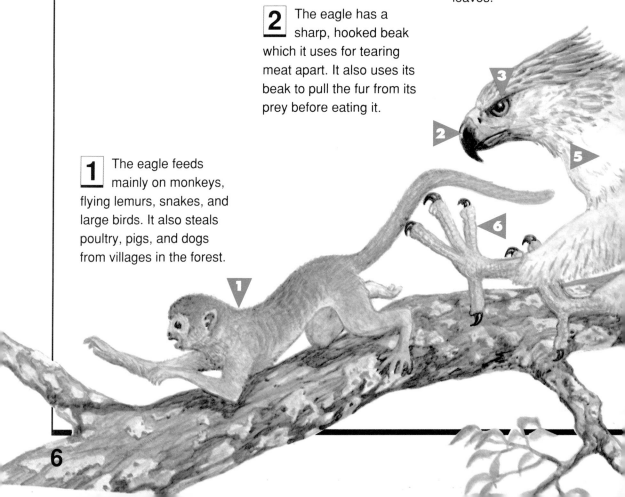

4 Jungle eagles can fly at up to 50 miles per hour (80 kph). Short, broad wings allow them to twist and turn among the trees.

5 The monkey-eating eagle is powerfully built. Females are bigger than males. They can reach 35 inches (90 cm) in length and can weigh about 22 pounds (10 kg).

6 The eagle's feet have sharp, curved claws. Once they grab hold of a monkey, there is very little chance of escape.

►Hummingbirds

Hummingbirds play a vital part in the ecology of the rain forests of South America. They help to pollinate flowers; in other words, they help to carry pollen from one flower to another so that seeds can develop and new plants can grow.

Hummingbirds feed on insects and sweet nectar, found deep inside the rain forest flowers. They hover in front of the flowers, beating their wings up to 20 times a second. They then probe into the flowers with their long, thin bills and lap up the nectar with their tubelike tongues.

3 The hummingbird's small size allows it to dart easily and quickly between the flowers. But it uses up lots of energy doing this and has to eat regularly.

2 A hummingbird beats its wings so quickly they make a humming sound. It is a great acrobat in the air. It can hover, fly forward and backward, and up and down.

1 Many hummingbirds have shiny green feathers, with patches of green and other colors on their heads or breasts. They look like tiny flying jewels.

4 As the hummingbird feeds, the feathers on its forehead get dusted in yellow pollen. Then this pollen rubs off on the next flower the bird feeds on and so helps to pollinate it.

5 Flowers that rely on birds to pollinate them are usually red, pink, or orange. This is because birds see these colors best.

6 The sword-billed hummingbird's bill is as long as its body. It fits perfectly inside the tube-shaped passionflowers whose nectar it feeds on.

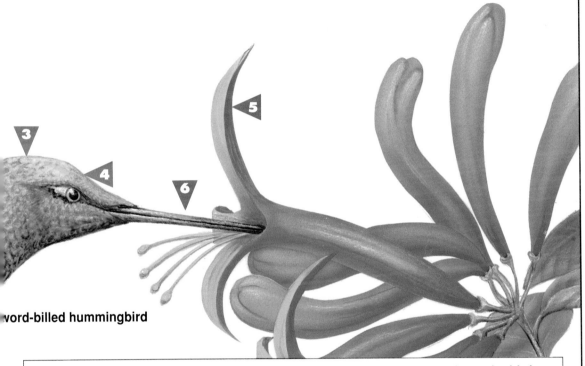

word-billed hummingbird

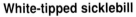

White-tipped sicklebill

The white-tipped sicklebill's curved bill is perfect for feeding on sickle-shaped flowers.

Giant hummingbird

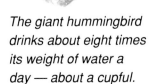

The giant hummingbird drinks about eight times its weight of water a day — about a cupful.

Bee hummingbird

The bee hummingbird is the world's smallest bird. It lays eggs no bigger than a pea.

9

Toucans

3 The bright colors of toucans' beaks probably act like signals to help them recognize each other. They may also help to scare other birds away.

2 Toucans eat fruit, berries, and some insects and spiders. First they pluck the berries, then they toss their heads back to throw the berries down their throats.

1 The toucan's long beak allows it to reach fruit growing on branches and twigs which are far away or too weak to bear the toucan's whole weight.

Toucans live in flocks in the Amazon rain forest. They are sociable, playful birds. One of their favorite games seems to be a type of wrestling, in which they try to push each other off the branch with their huge bills. They also preen each other with their bills.

Toucans build nests in holes high up in the tree trunks. These may be natural holes or nest holes stolen from woodpeckers. The toucans pull out any rotten wood to make the holes bigger and deeper. They lay between two and four white eggs which take about two weeks to hatch.

Toucans are famous for their large, brightly colored bills. The toco toucan, shown here, has the biggest bill of any toucan. It can grow up to 8 inches (20 cm) long, almost a third of the total length of the bird.

4 Toucans are poor fliers and only spend a short time in the air. They prefer to hop from branch to branch instead of flying.

5 Newborn toco toucans are blind and naked. They grow adult plumage gradually, which is mainly black, with some white and red feathers.

Toco toucan

6 Toucans have feet which are adapted for climbing. They have two toes pointing forward and two toes pointing backward. This provides a firm grip on the branch.

Macaws

Large, noisy flocks of parrots fly among the trees in the rain forests of Central and South America and Australia. Macaws are the largest types of parrots. The scarlet macaw can measure 35 inches (90 cm) from its head to the tip of its long tail. It is famous for its bright feathers. But many parrots have green plumage which helps to camouflage them in the jungle.

Parrots mainly eat fruit and seeds from the treetops. They will also feed on nectar and buds. Scarlet macaws gather regularly in large groups at certain places along the riverbank. They come to the riverbank to eat the soil which provides them with essential minerals.

Many types of parrots are endangered because the forests are being destroyed. They are also being collected, illegally, for the pet trade.

3 Although most large species of parrots fly more slowly than small ones, the narrow wings of the scarlet macaw make it a fast flier.

2 The scarlet macaw is named for its striking plumage. Its feathers are not only scarlet but also blue, yellow, and green. It preens its feathers with its bill.

1 Macaws have very long tails, which may make up over half of their total body length. They use their tails for signaling to other macaws and for braking as they land.

Scarlet macaw

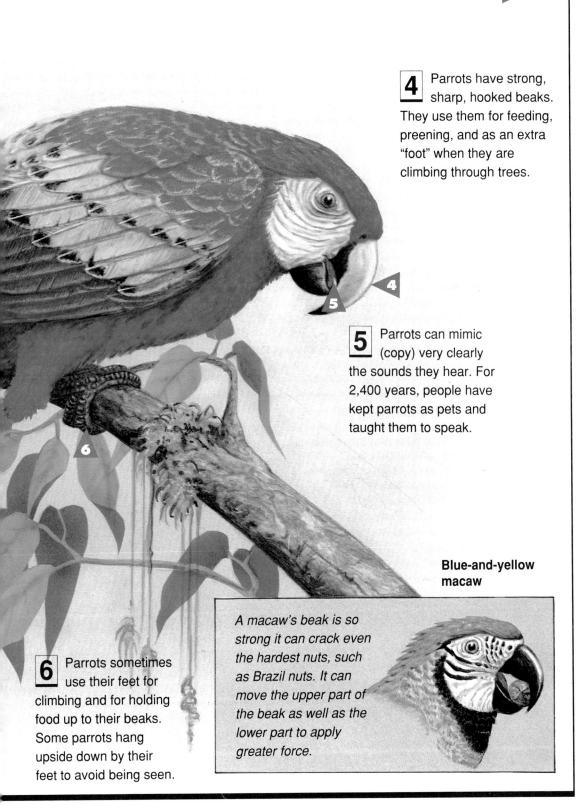

4 Parrots have strong, sharp, hooked beaks. They use them for feeding, preening, and as an extra "foot" when they are climbing through trees.

5 Parrots can mimic (copy) very clearly the sounds they hear. For 2,400 years, people have kept parrots as pets and taught them to speak.

Blue-and-yellow macaw

6 Parrots sometimes use their feet for climbing and for holding food up to their beaks. Some parrots hang upside down by their feet to avoid being seen.

A macaw's beak is so strong it can crack even the hardest nuts, such as Brazil nuts. It can move the upper part of the beak as well as the lower part to apply greater force.

Cassowaries

Cassowaries live in the jungles of Papua New Guinea and Australia. They are related to emus and ostriches. They cannot fly, but they can move speedily through the undergrowth on their long legs. Cassowaries are large birds. The cassowary shown here is as tall as an adult human.

Cassowaries eat fruit which has fallen from the trees, as well as insects, snails, and fungi. The birds are hunted for their meat by some of the rain forest tribes in Papua New Guinea. They kill them with bows and arrows. In some places, cassowaries are even raised on farms.

2 The strange, loose flaps of skin that hang down from the cassowary's bare neck are called wattles. These may be blue, red, or yellow. Wattles may be used for signaling.

1 Cassowaries have large, bony growths on their heads. These are called casques and are used for pushing through the undergrowth and for turning over leaf litter to find food.

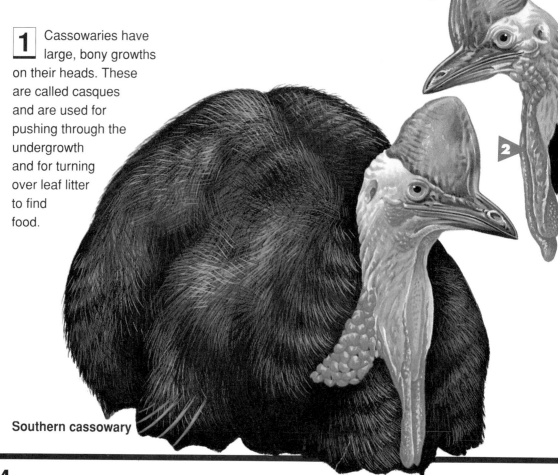

Southern cassowary

3 Cassowaries have black plumage. Their feathers hang downward, giving the birds a shaggy appearance.

Newborn cassowaries have dark- and light-brown striped plumage with white on their necks. They turn black as they grow.

4 The cassowary's wing feathers have large, spiky quills that help to protect the body as the bird moves in the jungle. They may also be used in self-defense.

5 Cassowaries have long, strong legs. If an enemy comes too close, a cassowary kicks out at it. It can kill with a single, well-aimed kick.

6 The cassowary has three toes on each foot, each with a dagger-sharp claw. These can cause terrible injuries.

Quetzals

With their glittering emerald-green and crimson feathers, quetzals are among the most brilliantly colored birds in the world. According to an old Central American Indian legend, they were once green all over. But their breast feathers became soaked in the blood of the Indians, killed when the Spanish conquered the region. The quetzal was once worshipped as the god of the air, and its beautiful tail feathers were highly valued for ceremonial costumes and headdresses. Today it is the national emblem of Guatemala, and the country's currency is named after the quetzal.

The quetzal lives in the rain forests of Central America and belongs to a group of birds called trogons. Large areas of its forest home have been cut down, and the bird is now very rare.

3 Quetzals particularly like the fruit of the ocotea tree. They swallow the fruit whole then spit out the large fruit stones later.

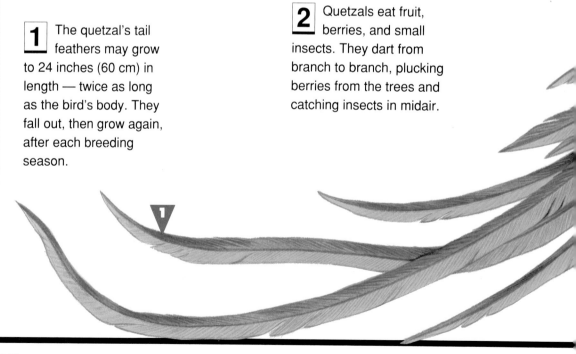

1 The quetzal's tail feathers may grow to 24 inches (60 cm) in length — twice as long as the bird's body. They fall out, then grow again, after each breeding season.

2 Quetzals eat fruit, berries, and small insects. They dart from branch to branch, plucking berries from the trees and catching insects in midair.

4 The quetzal has a spiky crest of short, bristlelike feathers on top of its head.

6 It is only the male quetzals that have stunning red and green feathers. Females are much more drab.

5 Quetzals fly up to the fruit and snatch it in midair. They then take the fruit back to a perch and eat it there.

◀

Quetzals lay their eggs in holes in tree trunks. The holes may have been wasp or ant nests. The male quetzal shares the duties of incubating the two light-blue eggs and feeding the chicks with the female.

Birds of Paradise

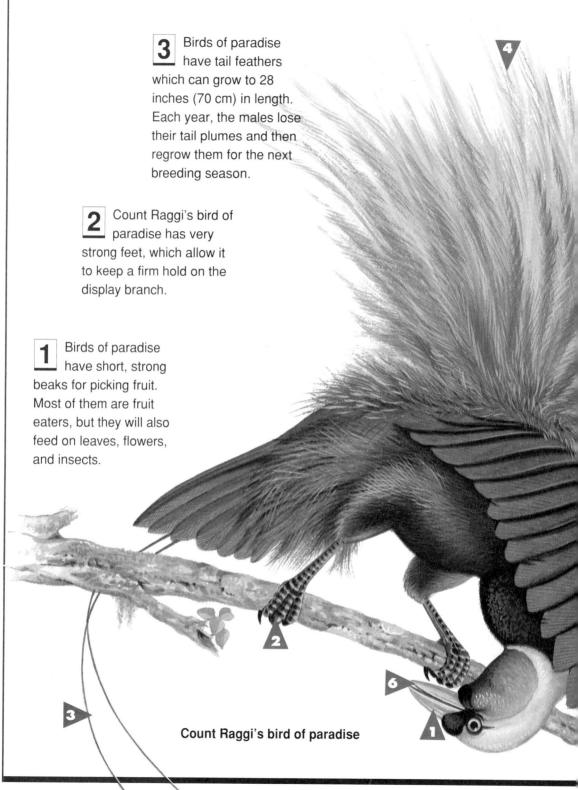

3 Birds of paradise have tail feathers which can grow to 28 inches (70 cm) in length. Each year, the males lose their tail plumes and then regrow them for the next breeding season.

2 Count Raggi's bird of paradise has very strong feet, which allow it to keep a firm hold on the display branch.

1 Birds of paradise have short, strong beaks for picking fruit. Most of them are fruit eaters, but they will also feed on leaves, flowers, and insects.

Count Raggi's bird of paradise

4 The male birds must spend a great deal of time and energy preening and displaying their beautiful feathers.

Birds of paradise got their name because of the amazing feathers and plumes of the male birds. When they were first discovered, people could not believe that such stunning creatures came from Earth. They believed that they must have come from paradise.

Birds of paradise live in Australia and Papua New Guinea. The males use their plumage to win the attention of females during the breeding season. Count Raggi's bird of paradise, shown here, puts on a special display to show off its feathers. Ten or so males display in the same tree. Females are very drab compared with the males. This is to camouflage them as they sit on their nests so that they are not seen by predators which might steal the eggs. The females mate with the male who puts on the best show.

5 Despite their beautiful appearance, birds of paradise are in fact related to the much duller-looking crows and starlings.

6 To attract a mate, the male makes loud noises like a cracked bell and often hangs upside down fanning out its tail plumes.

Honeyguides

3 Some types of honeyguides have ridge-shaped nostrils. They may use their sense of smell to help them find out where the bees' nests are located.

4 As the honeyguide leads the tribesmen to the bees, it flies along in a series of short swoops. It keeps stopping to let the people catch up.

2 The honeyguide needs help in breaking open bees' nests because its beak is too thin and fragile for such a tough task. It only uses its beak to probe for insects and wax.

Black-throated honeyguide

1 The black-throated honeyguide uses a special chattering call to guide people to the bees' nests. This is the only time it uses this particular call.

6 Like other climbers, the honeyguide has feet designed for gripping. The second and third toes of each foot point forward, and the first and fourth point backward.

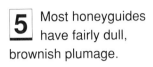

5 Most honeyguides have fairly dull, brownish plumage.

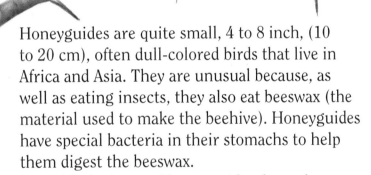

Honeyguides are quite small, 4 to 8 inch, (10 to 20 cm), often dull-colored birds that live in Africa and Asia. They are unusual because, as well as eating insects, they also eat beeswax (the material used to make the beehive). Honeyguides have special bacteria in their stomachs to help them digest the beeswax.

The black-throated honeyguide, shown here, is even more remarkable. Bees' nests are often difficult to break into. So the honeyguide gets people from the forest tribes to help it. It flies along, calling as it goes, and leads the tribesmen to the bees' nest. Then the men climb the tree and break the nest open. They collect the honey to eat and leave some for the bird. The bird also picks bee grubs and beeswax from the ruins of the nest to eat.

Pittas

Pittas are small, brightly colored birds which live on the rain forest floor in Southeast Asia. Their name comes from an Indian word for bird. Pittas spend most of their time foraging for snails, worms, and insects among the leaf litter. Some have a special stone which they use to break snail shells open. Pittas are rather shy, secretive birds. Many of them feed at night.

If danger threatens, pittas may hop or fly away, keeping close to the ground. Another method they have for defending themselves is to stand completely still, with their back toward the attacker. This makes them difficult to see among the undergrowth.

Blue-winged pitta

3 Some species of pittas have large eyes. Their eyes help them find food among the gloomy undergrowth and at night.

Noisy pitta

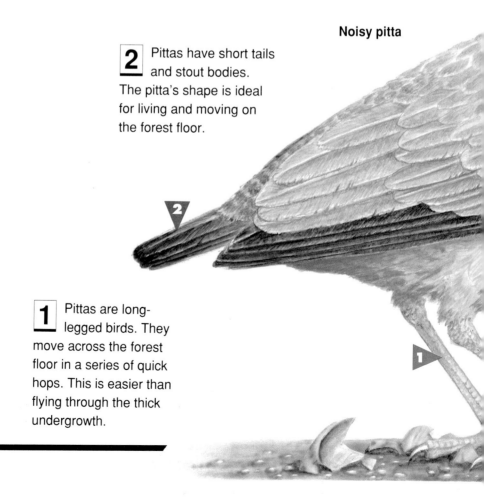

2 Pittas have short tails and stout bodies. The pitta's shape is ideal for living and moving on the forest floor.

1 Pittas are long-legged birds. They move across the forest floor in a series of quick hops. This is easier than flying through the thick undergrowth.

Some species of pitta, including the blue-winged pitta shown here, migrate each year. They travel at night, at the time of the new moon.

4 Pittas have a superb sense of smell. They use this sense to find food among the leaf litter and underground.

5 Pittas use their bills to poke and peck among the leaf litter for food. Hooded pittas dig for worms with their bills.

6 Pittas have a variety of plumage colors, depending on the species. The feathers may be bright blue, green, white, yellow, black, or red. Their plumage is usually the brightest on the underside, making them difficult to see from above.

Hornbills

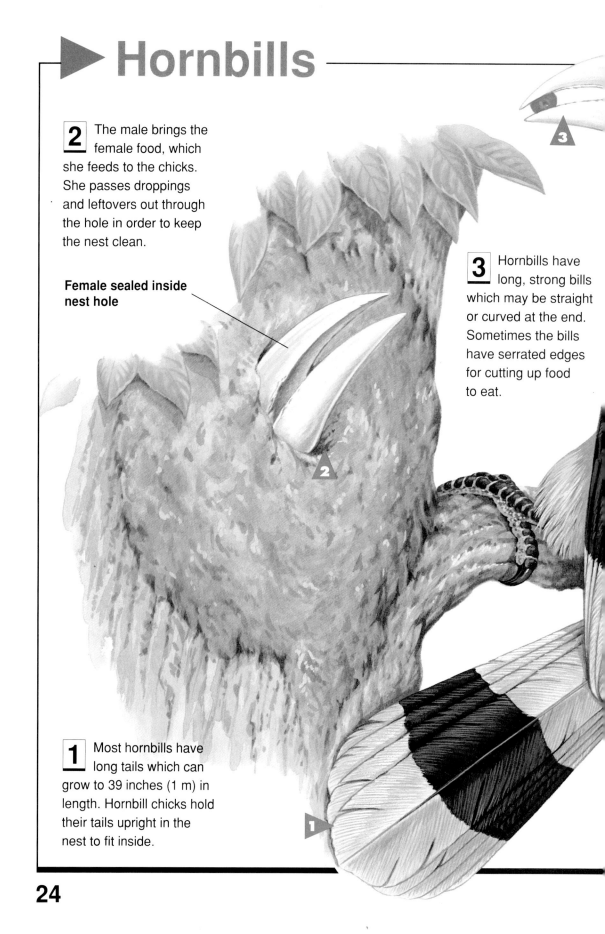

2 The male brings the female food, which she feeds to the chicks. She passes droppings and leftovers out through the hole in order to keep the nest clean.

Female sealed inside nest hole

3 Hornbills have long, strong bills which may be straight or curved at the end. Sometimes the bills have serrated edges for cutting up food to eat.

1 Most hornbills have long tails which can grow to 39 inches (1 m) in length. Hornbill chicks hold their tails upright in the nest to fit inside.

4 The big, bony growth on top of the hornbill's bill is called a casque. It may help to amplify sounds and calls. It may also help in recognition.

5 Hornbills smear oil from special glands, called preen glands, over their feathers to keep them in good condition. In the great hornbill, the oil is a yellowish color.

Great Indian hornbill

6 Hornbills have broad wings with gaps between the feathers. They make a whooshing sound in flight as air rushes through the gaps.

Hornbills are found mainly in India and Southeast Asia. They are easy to recognize — many have large "double-decker" bills which make them look top-heavy. They eat fruit and insects, as well as tree frogs and young birds. The great Indian hornbill is the largest hornbill. It grows to about 60 inches (1.5 m).

A female hornbill lays her eggs in a hole in a hollow tree. She then seals herself inside the hole with the eggs. Helped by the male, she covers the hole with mud and droppings. She leaves a tiny slit through which the male can deliver food but which is too small for snakes to enter. The chicks then hatch in safety. When the chicks are bigger, the female breaks out of the nest and helps the male to feed them.

Hoatzins

The hoatzin lives in South America. With its blue face, spiky head feathers, and long tail, it is one of the strangest-looking birds in the rain forest. It is about the size of a chicken but is in fact related to the cuckoo. A third of the hoatzin's weight is taken up by a huge crop. This is where the bird stores and digests the large amounts of plant food it eats.

Adult hoatzins are strict vegetarians, feeding on mangrove leaves, flowers, and buds. They live and feed among the tall trees which overhang the jungle rivers and lakes.

3 Hoatzins have large wings but cannot fly very well or fast because their flight muscles are too weak. They can only remain in the air for about 109 yards (100 m) before crash landing.

2 Because its claws are weak, the hoatzin uses its tail for support and to help it keep its balance among the branches of the trees.

Adult hoatzin

1 The hoatzin has stout legs and weak claws. It looks much more like a chicken than a type of cuckoo, to which it is related.

4 The hoatzin's spiky chestnut head feathers and bright-blue face give it a startled appearance.

5 With its short, stout beak, a hoatzin can quickly pluck the leaves from the mangrove trees to eat.

6 The hoatzin's strange peacocklike shape, with the rust-red underside and white-tipped wings and tail, is like no other jungle bird.

Hoatzin chick

▶ *A hoatzin chick has a dramatic way of defending itself. It leaps from its nest into the river below. When the danger is past, it slowly climbs back up the tree. It has tiny claws on the top of its wings to help it grip the tree trunk.*

Vangas

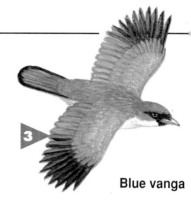

There are 14 species of vangas. Most species are found only on the island of Madagascar. (Just one species is also found on the Comoros Islands in the Indian Ocean). They are part of Madagascar's unique collection of wildlife which has evolved (developed) on the island since it broke off from the African mainland about 65 million years ago.

Each species of vanga has a different bill, which is designed for catching and eating a different type of food. Most vangas eat small creatures, such as insects, spiders, lizards, and snails.

Blue vanga

2 The nuthatch vanga is the smallest vanga. It measures about 6 inches (14 cm) in length. It has a distinctive red beak and a long claw on its first toe. The claw is used for pulling out grubs.

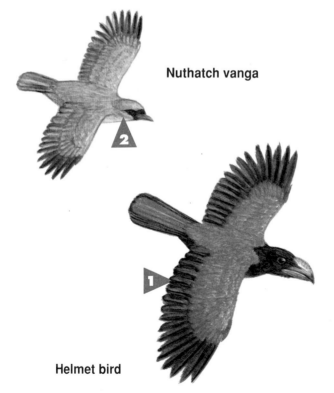

Nuthatch vanga

Helmet bird

1 The helmet bird has an amazing casque on its blue bill, which makes it look like a small hornbill.

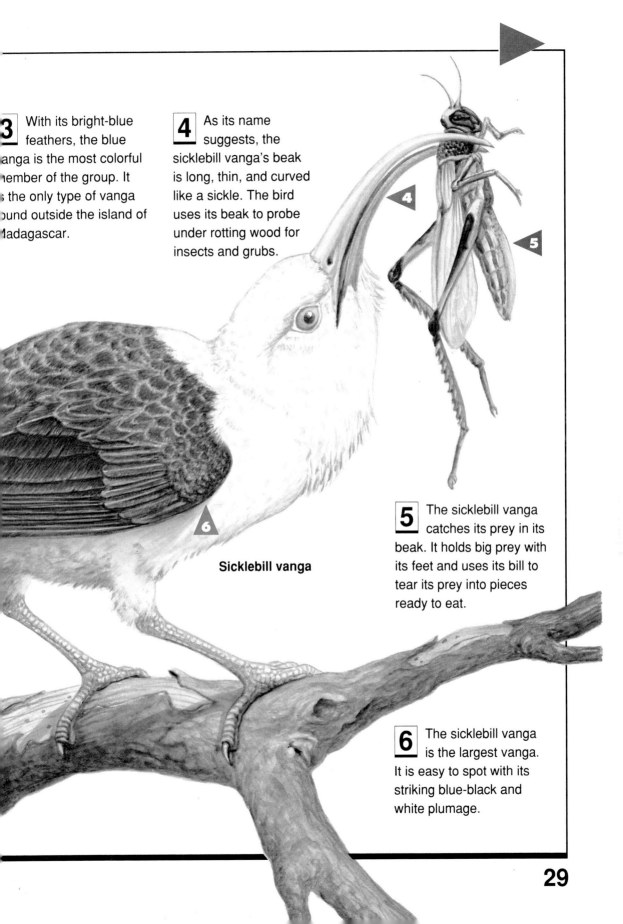

3 With its bright-blue feathers, the blue vanga is the most colorful member of the group. It is the only type of vanga found outside the island of Madagascar.

4 As its name suggests, the sicklebill vanga's beak is long, thin, and curved like a sickle. The bird uses its beak to probe under rotting wood for insects and grubs.

Sicklebill vanga

5 The sicklebill vanga catches its prey in its beak. It holds big prey with its feet and uses its bill to tear its prey into pieces ready to eat.

6 The sicklebill vanga is the largest vanga. It is easy to spot with its striking blue-black and white plumage.

▶ Glossary

Adaptations
Special features that help an animal to survive in its particular habitat. In a tree-dwelling bird, for example, this may include feet designed for climbing.

Amplify
To make louder

Bill
Another name for a bird's beak

Bird
A warm-blooded animal which breathes air. Birds lay eggs, usually in nests. They all have bills and are the only animals with feathers. All birds have wings, although not all can fly.

Bird of prey
A bird, such as an eagle, which is adapted for catching and eating meat. Birds of prey have hooked beaks, curved claws, and sharp eyesight.

Camouflage
Special markings or coloring which help to hide an animal in its surroundings.

Canopy
The thick layer of tree-tops which make up the "roof" of the rain forest. Most of the rain forest animals live here.

Casque
A bony growth on top of the bill of some birds, such as cassowaries

Crop
The enlarged part of a bird's gullet (food tube) where birds may store or partly digest their food

Crown
The top of a tree

Ecology
The study of the relationship between living things and their environment

Emergent layer
The tallest trees in the rain forest. They extend up above the canopy. Jungle eagles nest in the emergent layer.

Equator
An imaginary circle around the Earth which separates the north from the south

Flock
A large group of birds which tend to live and move in the jungle together

Incubation
The process by which birds keep their eggs warm, usually by sitting on them, so that the chicks grow and hatch properly. They need to be kept at a temperature of about 95°F (35°C).

Jungle
A name often given to rain forests, meaning a tangled mass of trees and other plants. The word *jungle* comes from a native word meaning forest.

Leaf litter
The layer of dead and rotting leaves which cover the forest floor

Migrate
To make long, regular journeys between breeding and feeding places at particular times of the year

30

Nectar
A sweet syrupy liquid made by plants and found at the base of a flower's petals

Nest
Cradles made by birds, usually from twigs and stems, in which they lay their eggs

Ocotea
A type of tree which is a member of the laurel family

Plumage
The feathers which cover a bird's body

Plume
Another word for a long feather

Pollen
Tiny, yellowish grains made by the male parts of a flower

Pollination
The process by which pollen from the male parts of a flower is carried to the female parts of a flower. It joins with the female parts to form a seed from which a new plant can grow.

Predator
An animal that hunts and feeds on other animals

Preen glands
A gland on a bird's body which produces oil. The bird smears the oil over its feathers with its beak to keep them in good condition. Not all birds have preen glands.

Preening
The way a bird keeps its feathers clean and in good condition using its beak

Prey
Animals that are hunted by other animals for food

Quill
A feather's hollow stem. A large wing or tail feather may also be called a quill.

Rain forest
The name given to the tropical forests which grow along the equator in Central and South America, Africa, Asia, and parts of Australia and Papua New Guinea. They cover less than 6 percent of the Earth's surface but are home to at least half of all the world's species of plants and animals.

Serrated
Something which has a notched or jagged edge, like the blade of a saw

Species
A group of animals that are all of the same kind. They look alike and live and behave in similar ways. They are able to breed with each other but not with other species.

Trogon
The group of jungle birds which includes quetzals

Troop
Another word for a group of animals, such as monkeys

Understory
The layer of smaller trees below the canopy

Warm-blooded
An animal whose body temperature tends to stay the same, even when the outside temperature changes

Index